Fish
Work
Caitlin
Maling

Caitlin Maling is a Western Australian poet whose previous collections, *Conversations I've Never Had* (2015), *Border Crossing* (2017) and *Fish Song* (2019) were published by Fremantle Press. In 2019 she was awarded her doctorate in literature from University of Sydney. Her poetry and non-fiction has been published widely through Australia, the US and the UK. She is the previous recipient of the Marten Bequest in poetry and grants from the Australia Council and the Department of Culture and the Arts, Western Australia.

Fish
Work
Caitlin
Maling

UWA PUBLISHING

First published in 2021 by
UWA Publishing
Crawley, Western Australia 6009
www.uwap.uwa.edu.au

UWAP is an imprint of UWA Publishing
a division of The University of Western Australia

ISBN: 978-1-76080-164-9

A catalogue record for this
book is available from the
National Library of Australia

Cover design by Sandy Cull
Typeset in Bembo by Lasertype
Printed by McPherson's Printing Group

This project has been assisted by the Australian Government through
the Australia Council, its arts funding and advisory body.

*To the crew at LIRS
and Charlie Maling,
the best research assistant
a person could want.*

There is skin. There is a slow thud.
There is hard. There are, at most, only fibres.
Once there were labels for this. For the parts
and how they come together. My mind.
I try to think of binds. I say this is your
corpse. These hands and feet and between. Then I
try to feel it all at once. This is the sum.
This is the sun.

Under the ocean we lay wires. Like fibres.
Not mine. Send men, me, in heavy suits to check them.
Bodies in oxygen, then rubber. No water. Water
on the outside. If you're fully in water
you can't see it. Everything blurs. But we see clearly,
separate. In the cement are wires. Inside wires
light. The bottom is dark. He/we/I carries a torch.
I can't step into the light. I'll keep
separate, steady. How can you measure light
but in speed. No mass. I am only mass.
And in the water, lower.

He/I under. She's out there. The only way to touch:
the wires. The light. He has his fibres to make him see her.
And she's there. In her fingers
threads. All bright colours. And him all over. In one panel
he fires an arrow. It's quill and thread crossing the whole.
Until the end. Where it reaches her.
The tube chinks. Each year the water gets warmer.
So far north, they used to crack the ice to let the fish breathe.

Now he's under an ocean open and rocking with the warm breath
of a mother bedding down an infant. It wasn't long
before the currents turned, sky clouded, no stars. The whales
turned circles and stopped singing. No gods came.

CONTENTS

with the coast on the right-hand side,
beaches like nails done in French tip for a wedding,
occasional fires rising from the brown crenelated ranges.
I swap seats to avoid the children
drumming some large creature's heartbeat on the back of my chair.
Below, a city appears because I turn and look for it.
Where I am going has only edges.
It is possible to walk and circle it in a day.
There is one incline, from it you can see the whole place laid out.
I have always wanted to be remote, a woman
cannot be an island but may aspire to it.
My eyes are not ice, rather the mist blue
of the horizon outside the plane window.
This is two and a half hours of figuring out
how to get somewhere, even though a boarding gate
assisted my choice; still I think I'm willing it,
the way the road from above cuts straight
from unseen place to shore across the lives
of others and other-than-humans burrowing and calling
beyond the hiss of the air keeping our empty places
at the right pressure so they feel full.

Symbiosis

I exchange books
for food, in terms
of the allocated weight
my case can carry:
a thin journal on infanticide
equals a pepper grinder,
the crime fiction paperback
with more pages than
its plot can support –
a jar of pickled peppers.

It's novel to get to enact
the radio, late night
or speed-dating game
of desert island. In all
things sustenance wins
but what form that takes
varies.

       I find I have bought
only cheap food and rich books
and need to scrounge for protein
and trash respectively.
In this regard, I'm a failure.
I haven't managed to provide
everything I need in a generous
impermeable case, but must rely
on others needing
what I have to offer.

Jose my Portuguese housemate does the PhD spiel –
thesis in 60 seconds:

>   he is here to take the cleaner fish from patches of reef
>   so the damselfish that need them become stressed.
>   Then, after a while, he catches those too,
>   keeps them in the tanks in the courtyard,
>   adjusts the water so it is hotter or more acidic than normal.

The theory is, that once you adjust to one thing
you're better equipped for more.

The Swiss Team

i.

The hot Swiss boy who has the longer hair,
the round glasses and is from the other house,
explains his two experiments
as we stand by the blue tubs
labelled AQUARIUM USE ONLY.

The first is the age old
what happens when we take the food away?

I'm more interested in learning that the fish
that come to be cleaned are called the client fish
and that one of the choices the cleaners make
is how to treat them:

> whether to nip parasitically
> to get at the best stuff
> or to softly nibble the ectoparasites
> from the smooth undersides;

a heady rush or
> the satiation of a heavy belly
> and the prospect of repeat custom.

ii.

When Jose starts to tell me of the second experiment
he blushes.

Apparently, the cleaner fish sometimes

(and at this he opens his fingers
   and brings them together one-by-one from the pinkie)

use their pectoral fins to give the clients a massage.

I don't know the purpose. Later when

he shows me the cleaner fish for the first time

I see their neon blue stripes, and he says

all over the world cleaners have the same blue and yellow.

   Yes, I think,

just like a red light above a door

in Bangkok, or Melbourne.

         And I know, I'm making

things too human again. But see

how the Swiss boy blushes, his fingers

attempting to dance scientifically, objectively,

a motion none of us can know

but know anyway.

It's also true

that I make everything a story,

and this is one of me watching those fingers

on an island where the wind never stops blowing sou-easterly,

my husband still safely in bed

thousands of kilometres south.

This is the Poem Written on the Only Dry Bits of Paper Locked in a Sandwich Bag Under My Wetsuit

I must get used to sharks
But there are differences in knowing
the white tips never bite
and the black tips only when provoked

and that silver skin
5 metres away
moving with swift sharp
flicks of the tail
'they don't bite
until they do' tattooed
between pectoral fins
like 'Loyalty and Family'
between the pecs of a Bra Boy

I swim in to the beach
on a glazed calm day
sandwich bag with book, paper and biscuit
wedged under my wetsuit

I'm only a coward
when I'm over the sandy patch
the grey sky turning
every direction

to cream and shadow

Jose Tells Me a Story About Cleaner Fish

After I tell the Portuguese I'm writing poems about cleaner fish,
Jose asks if I want to know how he fell in love with the ocean.
He will, he says, tell me a story about the cleaner fish.

With a wink Tiago says this is the story he tells all the girls,
so I'm expecting something salacious
but what follows is fairy tale.

When Jose was younger, no more than about 8,
he got a book from the library, or perhaps
it was an Xmas present, but either way
it was a Big Book of Fish and he fell in love
(& at this his voice deepens towards
some other fathom of emotion) with the symbiosis
between cleaner and client, the mutualism.

This wouldn't work for me if I was a girl in a bar.

I'd think about the cleaners, their colours, their dancing fins,
how the client does nothing but lug its body over to the rock
and allow itself to be cleaned. I'd wonder if the cleaners
clean each other. If the parasites that attach
to even small damselfish, avoid them for meatier prey.

Or, if in some other natural heartbreak,
the blue and yellow they flash like placards
attract fish but tell their food to stay back.

But these flights into human imagination are unfair of me.
Jose, while telling this story, has his eyes half-closed,
his body openly angled as if he too is being cleaned,
or has just eaten enough to be full.

Lit Review

At dinner, I meet the last of the Swiss team:
>the impossibly beautiful girl
>and the boy who spends all his time in the library
>talking to a girl somewhere else in the world.

Her fish can count
>or at least tell the difference between 5 and 8 dots
>drawn in black on white squares.

This, they were not expecting,
nor the fact that there are dumb and smart fish.

Some that can complete these tasks
>and some that can't.

The ones that can, they say,
>'just want it more.'

I ask if our Australian cleaners
are smarter or stupider

and the answer is,
>'they just seem more stressed.'

She tells me, 'in all seriousness
>it's a difference in attitude.'

I ask, as expected,
>'is it the reef?'

At that we follow the pattern:
        bleaching – devastating;
        80% of coral gone
        and apparently 80% of the cleaners.

In the 12 months of the cyclones and "the event"
instead of harvesting the brains of the cleaner fish
the Swiss let them go
so that there'd be a few of them left.

She doesn't know if those that are gone
    swam for better waters
            the southern patches of coral
or, if confused,
            they couldn't find their homes
            and so just kept swimming

aimlessly
        to their deaths.

I Try to Get Used to the Reef

At Mermaid Cove I stay where the depth
keeps me brushing my belly against the bombies.

It's true that the north side of the cove is rubble
and the south just has some pieces barely lit up

by the right kind of algae. Still here are fish
darting in and out of the wreckage.

Some leave plumes of sand when startled.
In the calm water there's a presence

like a ghost in the unsettled grains. I keep
thinking maybe we can learn from these fish

about how to survive what's coming,
but I'm here now seeing many

whereas others, who return year after year
are seeing fewer.

Amongst these fish there's no war for resources.
No sudden desire for the taste of their own flesh.

The salt and oxygen content of the water stays
the same. I am still buoyant

enjoying the warmth of the water
against my skin.

At lunch I ask,

     'Jose what does a cleaner fish look like to you?'

He says:

     'They are slim, blue and yellow
     and they dance,'

and at this he does, too, hands by his chest,
pointing out, bouncing foot to foot.

See, I say, see

I ask Tiago

what a cleaner fish looks like to him

'Nothing,' he says,

     'I don't like them.'

This is What a Cleaner Fish of the Species *Labroides dimidiatus* Looks Like to Me

Like a pinkie finger animated
Like an animated pinkie someone has taken a blue marker to

Like a misshapen butterfly

Like a cartoon fish
                    shrunk down from the big screen

Like it's always saying 'Hi'
           and waving, 'I'm over here'

Like it's never lonely

Like it has put on so much makeup
           to looks as if it is never lonely

Like it's dancing in a non-concerned
           over-the-shoulder come hither

Like if you bumped against it
           it'll grind back on you

Like it's permanently hungry

Like it's always in need

After the black tip
appears in the 1m water
and swims in circles around me
I return to the beach,
climb onto the only patch of shade
on the rocks

When I'm in the water
I try to focus
on my loneliness,
so much so that when
the shark appears I'm startled

You won't believe this, but
as I write these words
there's a splash in the water
right by the current line
leading to the beach
and I watch two juvie sharks
chase something down
to the foot of the rocks
where I'm perched, still sunburnt

I've been told
this is the channel
everything that comes
must pass through here
which includes me
on my inevitable swim
back to the boat

For now I sit and watch
snails I've never seen before
move slowly
with antennae extended
feeling out a home,
approaching my feet
like land

Aye, There's the Rub

There's no undercurrent of cruelty
when Jose takes the fish in his hands
from respirator to beaker to scale to beaker again.
'I'd rather touch fish than most people,' he says.
Yet he is not kind with them.
He swears as they flop out of his hand
and miss the upturned jar while he calls out
numbers in Portuguese to Tiago.
I hover like a sand fly at their heels.

On the boat, Jose says the girl he loves
left him because of his work.
I wonder what it's like to be excluded from that focus.
If my husband feels that way when I'm here,
or when he sees my silent hand wrangling,
the placing and dropping of words.

Loomis

I sit this one out, in the kitchen
thinking of my husband. It takes a lot
not to try and fix people and he manages
on the phone, to listen to the same problems
he's been listening to for 15 years
and only sometimes do I sense he's taken
his mind back to the task I've interrupted
'it's like this', I say, and he patiently
takes apart the knot I've twisted
hands it back to me and says
'try again'.

Something About It Says — Speak Softly

i.

A personal tragedy
on top of a national one,
my old home city floods
while one of my home people
is done out of a dream
by a classified ad in the paper.

I sit on the deck.
Watch the palm tree,
the shades of blue
in the water,
the almost flat top
of the other island.

Something in me
knows that this
is winter,
even as I prep
my suit, snorkel, mask and fins
for the almost tepid water.

ii.

I Google:
        boat sale scam, Port Hedland.
It's the first result.
        Mum is barely holding it together
and will not answer questions.

I know this is not the tragedy
　　　　but the inciting incident.
We weigh our words like stones
　　　　placing them carefully to the ground.

iii.

Mum won't tell us what happened.
I imagine, when I close my eyes
and listen, that the sound coming off the ocean –
the Eastern Trade Winds in the casuarinas,
the melody of locust wings –
is her sadness.

I hold it to my ear
like a conch shell.
I do not mind
if something crawls out
of fluorescent blue whirls
and eight-legged danger.

We were always told
to leave the things we found
on the ocean floor,
to not overturn stones.

On the phone, she says,
'leave it Caitlin, just leave it.'

We climb Cook's Look
and the Portuguese film each other

while I try to stay out of sight lines.
Something has ruptured in our comfortable three.

I return sunburned and dizzy
and the next day twist my ankle on the boat

retire to the couch and cry.

The boys sleep early and return
to their slow culling of fish.

Letter from Palfrey

I watch the dark patch of wind
move like another boat
across the surface,
my ankle swelling like a puffer fish.
I'm not an easy person,
I know this, but for now, I am alone,
the only person on this rocky shore
I've hobbled myself onto
with my one good foot
and half good heart.

This is not a metaphor:
the tide coming in,
how I am lonely
for my loneliness,
the pang of knowing
who I'm lonely for.

Out in the water
one of the men surfaces
struggling with the shallow depth
to keep to the bottom.
I imagine I'm a stone,
my hard ankle and harder heart
only hurting when I force them
to move.

Team after team
comes to study the ground.

The American might live on the island
for a year straight, take a boat
out each day to see what use the reef
makes of the grit and ground water
washed out by the tide and rain.

Each day at 6 am
my new housemates
leave for South Island to dig.
A shell midden appears
cm by cm. On a good day
they might get down the depth
of the fingers on my right hand.

The team from WA, who appeared last night,
use the tractor to lower a compressor to their boat,
to drill and core and age the *porites*.

These are all solid people.
Practical. Go to bed early.
Each of them needs to be capable
of looking at the dirt they hold
and saying it is millions of years
beyond our knowing. Understanding
that everything we learn
can never be held by parchment,
stone, iron filings or light.

Each day they practise
with the time we have,
sweeping, filtering and drilling
a small window into earth.

Naive Lizard

Varanus panoptes

i.

A team comes to study
    if the lizards here
    move differently
    from mainland goanna

We are in the east
    where every monitor
        is a goanna

and these are slow ones
    stumbling over the motion
        of their own joints

Only when startled
    into a run
    do the parts
        seem to come together

coalesce into the sloping pen
    Goanna writes with in elegant cursive
        a series of arches
            on the sand

that have me looking for snakes
    every time I cross paths
        until I notice
        the tail

trailing surely behind
like a brush
laden with ink

ii.

There are no cane toads here

on which the mainland lizards

grow sour, cynical and dead

The team tests whether the venom

means anything to our goannas,

makes them stop in their tracks

One thing I've been wondering

is whether the bones of the coral

are relevant to the lizard, which keeps

to the sand amid the frogs and large insects

that appear on the wind

                         Sometimes

the lizards stick out their tongues and raise

a bubble of air in their throats, stand

still as a sleeping cow and wait

for me to pass, even at 100 m

I see this stillness settle over them

It wouldn't be hard to believe

that the air blowing up

off the worst parts of the reef

is necrotic with dead coral

even though the water stays

that sharp and deadly glass blue

iii.

A thing I know well
is to stay out of direct sun
between hours 10–3 or even 9–4

I still on the shaded verandah
Am no threat to what waits in the sun
on the rock, cold blooded

each of us exchanging blood with air

iv.

After asking my husband if he's seen a lizard tripod yet
    I say *Varanus panoptes* is a large weight
       to put on any creature
                I know from my library time
panoptes is many eyes
and this is the monitor named for Argus:

    the 100 eyed giant set by Hera
    to guard Io transformed into a bovine
    until he was slain by Hermes
    who Zeus sent to free his lover-cow

    Disguised as a shepherd,
    and after singing each eye to sleep,
    Hermes brought the rock down on Argus's head
    introducing murder to a new generation of gods

These lizards are ancient.
Captain Cook named this island after them
noting in his journal that there seemed to be 'nothing
on this island but lizards' as he stood
watching over the fires of the Dingall nation

v.

To tripod, the reptile rises up
on its rear legs and tail.
It can rotate its head,
adjust its tongue
to make an aperture for food

All across its body, are yellow dots
much smaller than its eyes
which are dark and possibly
without lids

You can never get close enough
to tell

Kangaroo Country

'For most of the past two million years or so, the region we know
as the GBR would in fact have looked more like a modern-day
cattle station – kangaroo country – than a coral reef.'
J. E. N. Vernon *A Reef In Time* 135

But there would've been no fences,
no stockmen, no stolen land,
no massacre site two gullies over
never spoken about but which makes
its way into the water supply
through a bloodily named creek.

There wouldn't be cows munching
buffalo grass on acres of dry land
and there wouldn't be kangaroos
finding the one patch of shade
and timing their breeding cycles
for seasons of plenty

and plaguing when the cleared land
gives way to grass and wheat
after an unkind long wet season
so the pollies advocate importing
fast-firing bump-stock as a way
to cull the roos and preserve the harvest.

And there has never been, till now, the joy
of holding down a trigger and hearing
the consistent *thwack thwack thwack*
through your noise cancelling headphones,
like hearing against your mask and snorkel
a turtle hitting hard at a seagrass bed,

turtles of course being one of the few
that survived the rollercoaster of the Cenozoic era
evolving with the ability to eat anything
and to follow both warm and cold currents
as they narrow and widen
though even they won't survive

the atmospheric climb to $900\,ppm\ CO_2$
when the phytoplankton in the deep-sea fades,
then the krill, then the whole southern-ocean
sea-web except for maybe the algae,
growing up and over the bones
so it all looks, again, like a paddock.

let's be brutal

swim with your mouth open
tongue against the lips
of the snorkel

maybe you'll bite
the plastic till it tears

trace
the ragged grove

these rocks
this overhang

you want a current
to fight

to let your palms
slip on the molluscs

behind you
anything might
nibble

the way
the cleaners

put their heads
in the mouth
of the parrot fish

& trust
them not to
bite

Results

The fish smell is overwhelming.

They cut in Portuguese, the

    cérebro
    fígado
    brânquias
    músculo
    olhos
    intestino
    bílis
    rabo

labelled 1-8 neatly on a small white board.

Beheaded I cannot tell what fish this is.

Only that it is dead and there are 96 more to go.

Tiago says they are lucky to have had only a 1% mortality rate in the tanks.

Soon these too will be under the knife,

parcelled off, frozen, dispatched north.

I do not know why the outcome of the experiment matters.

Once, Tiago gets sick of cleaner fish talk over dinner

and asks why they are important

but Jose says with that half-hidden hardness he has

'they matter.'

Tiago throws his hands over his head

says, 'you might as well say all fish matter, cows matter, horses matter
parrots matter, you could even say that humans matter.'

Yes. I think.

You could.

Piscatory Eclogue

for Tiago Repolho (Cabbage)

With the four lines deep across his forehead
that indicates he's serious, Tiago tells me about
'the most important discovery in aquaculture.'

This is part of a conversation
about what he terms simple things:
'marriage, children, family.'

The hard membrane around the fluid sac of the brine shrimp
is called corion. 'It sounds like the sun,' I say, 'or at least
a star.' 'Maybe,' he says, 'but that's not what is important.'

What's important is the simple accident of a cleaning lady
putting bleach in a lab and the experimenter returning
to find the membrane gone, the shrimp free and soft to the touch.

'This means,' Tiago says, 'that now the fish can eat the shrimp'
without the hard, shattering star tearing at their throat.
'A simple thing,' he says, and what it means is more food.

'Why,' he says, 'do we send one man to look at a rock
on some far heavenly body when at home
20% of people live on bread and water.'

Tiago is a man of balanced heavens,
who does not take his head from the earth
where he thinks of the shrimp and the fish and the urchins,

not for their shape, the words they make in the mouth,
but for what they might deliver, simply,
with a little bread and water

to a marriage, children, family.

From What We Have Come to Sea

i.

From the start we know
it will come to nought.

I read *Tess of the D'Urbevilles*
at the Cairns aquarium, really
she allows them to be cruel to her.

The freshwater sawfish
has been banging its teeth
on the glass,

smudged fingerprints
prevent us seeing the scars.
At the end,

Tess wanders the flat moors
but here the tanks are oval,
you can only swim in circles.

She lies down and it turns out
it's on the altar stone where
'her breath quickens'.

We never see what fish breathe out
the pillar tanks trick the eye
so there's nowhere to run.

ii.

First day back in the water
or rather, first day ever
in this water, .06 m spring tide
swarming overnight from 1.94 m.
We walk 100 m offshore,
still ankle-deep in water, strap on gear
       push off.

Not everything that happens
on the reef is spectacular,
especially now, this far north.

Everyone takes destruction
in their own way. I look
for the places where the *acropora*
has started to regrow –
purple – more fingers
than you might picture on hands.
But these are not fingers
but branches. They don't end in leaves
but keep branching
for just as long
as the colour lasts.

iii.

In her essay *The Long Goodbye,*
Anna Krien tries to make us feel
what it's like for the earth
to warm an extra 2 degrees
by getting us to imagine ourselves
bedridden with fever.
As I read,
I am on the couch
using a cup of coffee
trying to make my chest
give up its ghost;
wherever I place the round
of warmth, my attention draws
away from the heaviness
at chest, nose and throat.
We get hot
from fighting off
infection. It seems too easy
to say the infection is us.

iv.

Once the oceans
were warm and soupy,
slimy even:
the coughed-up night
of someone getting over a cold.

In one of these mucous dead spots,
a diver feels a ghost pass over,
the tantalising sense
of something other than water.

Outfront,
where even 30 knots
struggles to raise a froth,
a man drowns at low tide.

We speculate:
something wrong with his heart,
a sting the autopsy doesn't pick up;
we take for granted,
how easy the water slides off us,
how little we fight to be
the lightest and highest
of all.

v.

It's hard to write poems among the people
moving and calling out at breakfast.

The clink of spoon on coralline –
sounds like ceramic but doesn't break when dropped.

Everything is sturdy in bright monochrome,
each house the same.

Yet they fall apart differently
face different angles to the weather –

an inconsistent hive – discrete corals
hanging in the vast water, beyond

where we ask each other if we slept ok,
talk about the winds and tides,

find patterns. Outside a glory of green
rustles, un-nameable things flit and float.

When we fly out, we see the reef in blocks
like paint-by-numbers, something deeper than white

like the arc of a fingernail growing out.
Underneath there are paint strokes and bristles

still moving, there will be some that survive and some
that drift, become lost in the benthic algae

which goes up and around, the same mud green
my mother uses to spray all the fences

around every house where we've ever lived.

vi.

It'll stop eventually.
Yet the trees stay bent
to 20 degrees and the whitecaps form
in the small television window of ocean.
We take out along the point with the wind,
which isn't necessarily easy
just easier than coming back will be,
the Tradewinds moving current-wise
with the South Pacific Gyre.
We go to Mermaid's Cove where it's all
fallen to rubble, monochrome
like a black and white fantasia –
a cross of the *Red Shoes* and Disney.
Something large has danced here
and not stopped dancing.
We expect rest you see,
even coral, but the thermocline,
the sun, the current, the tarantella
of syllables El Niño, La Niña,
the coral turns white and whiter,
then the turf algae comes – green –
like the end of the roll of film unspooling
or immolating, bright with mercury.

vii.

Coral cored
is a different way
of time-telling,
but from the surface
the *porites* whole
look like nothing else
but the blown-up-bulbs
of a daisies. Everything comes
back to flowers and these
are the Clam Gardens after all,
with their garish purple lips
and spotted neon green.
Living reefs are indecent,
over-abundant, you are always
swimming through spawn,
pulling up things clinging to the anchor-line.
The coral cored and scored
is a limestone plinth in miniature,
no war dead but rings
going back in century increments.
The reef bleached from space
would look like a jawbone
in the process of swallowing
half the world.

viii.

Even if the reef is dying
no one of us
will see all of it.

The span of our lives
fits easily
into the song of its death.

ix.

For a coral reef to grow
the skeletons of their dead
must be converted into solid rock

creeping on average
.6m per century

while the living *porites*
grows outward like an ageing stars
a cm per year

and the staghorns and plateforming *acropora*
stretch upwards and outwards
each the length of a child's ruler.

On the GBR only on one night,
within the same few hours,
following an October or November full moon

do the corals release their gametes,
a mass of slack egg and sperm bundles

that turn the water column pink
like the trapped reflection
of a falling meteor.

x.

A death is not singular
but many moments
of snuffed out matches,

and to think, it is only
60 years since the first
commercial underwater camera

allowed a select few
to take the reef home with them
and the rest of us

picked up magazines
and the human world
breathed in

in wonder.

They must measure
precisely at intervals
how many parasites remain
on each damselfish.

The damsels are in beakers.
Once devoid of parasites
they are returned to the respirator,
their oxygen levels taken.

The boys get up at 6 am
and sleep at 1 am.
They are tired
and snap at one another.

I try to say nice things,
dance around the kitchen,
count their specks of darkness
until they lift.

Northerly

Permit me to tell you
what happens when the wind changes:
the large palm by the bathroom
turns circles on its trunk
knocking coconuts together
like maracas, the trees straight ahead
by the ocean unbend
from their push rightwards,
although the leaves hang
still to that side
like an ox unyoked
that fears any sudden measures
might lead not to reyoking
but the recognition of pain
in every muscle
come from pushing relentlessly
in the singular direction forwards.

The thicket of weeds rustles as usual.
But, closing your eyes, you perceive
something has changed in the sound
of the whole like cathedral bells
with their ropes altered
so they chime on the hour
in a different register.
You are still aware
you are in the day
and you know to say
what day it is,

but the time is unfamiliar
as biting into baked ham
you think is treated with salt
and finding sugar instead.

Sunset: Ontogeny of Cooperation

Jose says I cannot sit at the table
because it shakes his camera and tripod.
He's filming the sunset
and singing Bon Iver –
his theme music
because it sounds one way
and means another. To get Jose
to talk, I must ask questions
about his work which makes him
excited as a seal even though I am –
to the Portuguese – the manatee.
Any man I try and make talk like this
is a man not interested in talking.
Still, Jose does better than most
answering what his fishwork means to him
as the spring tide rolls back up the beach.

A day later, it begins to rain.
Another sunset, slightly damper, Jose and I sit
wanting to feel the way we imagine
ourselves to be. Today he talks freely
and I do not know why he's telling me these things,
except perhaps I've made myself too good a mimic,
a fangbelly that pretends to clean
just to get at the flesh. I am disappointed
at so ordinary a thing as heartbreak,
so I change the subject, ask Jose
about the inadequacy of applying
human models to fish and he says evolution
means human is as much fish as fish is human.

Jose doesn't say I ask too many questions
but does say he prefers to wait, let things come out
naturally. He doesn't understand
that under all worlds there's silence
into which I order my syllables
like specimen bags.

Asymmetric Partnership Arrangements

After many days I get tired
of dancing around the Portuguese
and expecting them to feed me.

All cleaners start out
female and only change to male
when they take more
than their fair share
of food.

Most male cleaners
have at least three female partners
who they allow to eat
their leftover scraps.

He punishes her
if she grows too big
or keeps the best parts
for herself.

He will, the report says,
chase her
aggressively.

I have no fight
or flight response
and will
just stand here
in the face
of threat or
tumble
to the ground.

I wish I could say
my ecological niche
had gifted me
the skills to escape
the sudden pounding
my heart does
when I hear the door
crack open
and your footsteps
enter softly.

An Oversaturation of Clove Oil

I'm starting to feel for the clients.
Today when I enter the lab it smells like
over-brewed chai. I've asked how they kill the damsels
and the answer is a solution in the off-green
of last season's on-trend nail polish.

Clove oil, what dentists used
in past centuries to numb the gums. I ask Jose
what happens to the fish and he points to his board.
I hadn't realised he had a damsel there, laid out.

Underwater, these are not remarkable fish
I think of them as the mice of the fish world
because they're always in the labs
having things done to them in shoebox aquaria.

The dead fish no longer have even the slightest silver.
Their scleras are glazed. I now know
what the experiment is for, but I won't tell you
yet. You need to absorb the bodies

taken apart, put into test tubes like a fantasy
of a drug lab. One night, Tiago threatens
to enter my room, have Jose hold me down
and force-feed me ice-cream. I imagine the cold

spreading down my throat, up behind my eyes
while my wrists tighten and go slack,
but I already know what it means
to be numb.

Everyone Shares First Jobs by the BBQ

No one says breathing. There's
tractors and factories and Woolies,
caring for other people's children,
the itchy polyester of 1970s front-of-house.

One of the directors talks of a factory at Crow's Nest
putting pills into Webster-paks,
the satisfying hiss of the iron sealing them.

She lasted five days before the boredom set it
and yet she says 'there were people there
who'd worked for 20 years.' Of course all
those jobs are gone now.

                    But not Callie in the lab
pipetting solutions 10 hours a day
or adjusting the dial every 15 minutes so the fish
acclimatise slowly.

She tells me the ocean can never die
because it is always just water
but what lives in it might.

In every routine we make order
and in order faith.

In the library, the marine ecosystem charts
begin on the earth's surface,
with the mega-fauna and us,
then go deep into the sand of the seabeds
where micro-organisms

hold the carbon tightly,
like an inhaled breath
we are scared will be let go
all at once.

At the Bottom of It, Pain

Callie tries to give the fish a good death,
short and sharp, severing the brain stem.
Pithing – like the sound a cherry makes
when you extract the pip. Some things
are instinct like spitting out
what cracks, hard, against your teeth,
or how a fusilier in the net arches
its whole body like a rictus grin
when the fruit is sour.

I Tell Tiago My Oldest Heartbreak Over Lunch

There are aggressive and defensive mimics:
ones that looks more like the cleaners
and ones that don't. I'm never sure
which one I am: cleaner, client, aggressive, defensive.
There's a theory that we only say and think "I"
so we're solid enough to move
about the world. I could be a school,
a cluster. Often, I sense the presence
of an audience and the different parts of me
compete to perform or hide.
Soon, I shall be alone again
and then the chorus shall begin.

My husband flies to join me
so we can be the two worst campers
at science camp, where it seems
everyone knows more about the ocean
than it's possible for me to learn
even if I read all the pages
collected neatly in the library binders.

Tessa in the lab next door
is working on calcified coralline algae.
We spend a long time listening
to her explain what she does to the algae
before we learn that this isn't what floats
and fronds or washes up in soft clumps
but is hard, a rock that grows
and breathes and breeds.

Today she has been making it mate
with the ruthlessness of a cult leader in a movie.
First it must be scrubbed clean,
left alone overnight, out of water, in a cold dark room
before being dried, put back in water
and stored for six hours in sunlight.

The cult movie would, of course,
not be about the cult, but a metaphor
for some sightless violence that occurs
in the spaces between people. A concept.

What pushes out the tetra-spores in their 4x4
Tessa calls conceptacles, she shows us
the even dots of spores leading away
from the pin pricks from which they have been ejected
while we sit at sunset, G + T + lime in hand.

Why does she do it? My husband wants to know,
as if there is always a higher purpose and yet
there isn't. Tessa studies the algae for the algae.
Can draw on the whiteboard with exactness
their regular, straight, ancient cells.

Scientists, says the chapter on scientific language,
use metaphors only to explain what cannot be seen
or what cannot be understood, except by those
who spend their days as Tessa does,
looking closely and moving intimately with parts unseen,
the small details that accumulate into dust, a leaf
or even the reef, hard and protecting us all
like a calcified shell about our warming membranes.
Forgive me, I am a poet.

He will tell me I have the colours wrong,
the umlauts left out. That they
take the head after the fins.
That there isn't a fin at all
but some internal organ. Why
it matters if I specify
exactly what damselfish,
what cleaner and that this is
the Pacific ocean and an ocean
is not a sea.
                    A poet,
so many write, should always
be a truth teller.

                    I told Jose two days ago
I did not want to know the why
of the experiment, just what happened.
He asks me to repeat what I remember
 about what they are doing in the lab
and I do.

                    He says I am close.

Jose holds the parts of himself
at arm's length
as though keeping distance
from a mirror. But
with the fish
he is always
trying to get
closer.

Other Fish Aren't Capable of Feeding Against Their Preference

I listen to people talk about
their type; thick ass,
bearded; one friend

only likes men
with an ironic wit
who can out-talk her.

A truth I've long known
is that I could fall in love
with any man who touches me.

It is good
evolutionarily-wise
to be adaptive.

In one experiment,
they find the cleaners
learn to make the most

of their options,
While another wrasse
insistently feeds

on what
will always
be taken away.

A Bit of a Cold Fish

I want to write a poem
that can make a man love me.

Instead I have the fish,
or they have me watching them

without telling me their names,
diets,habits or what reef

they fell from. I trace the places
I would like to be touched

on my reflection in the aquaria:
just above my hip-bone, bare skin

on a day I smell like lilac, jasmine,
not sunscreen with a touch of salt.

Fish are softer than you would suppose,
supple, warmer and surprisingly sympathetic

to your angry litany of desires and eager
as always for the taste of you,

coming to nibble the finger you dangle
against experimental conditions.

There's power in that, choosing
exactly how much to give.

(I realise that as I've been writing these poems, I've been engaged with watching the first season of *The Girlfriend Experience*, a show where a law student accepts escort work to pay for school. Mostly there are shots of her face, her walking and her having sex.

When Jose and Tiago film the fish they zoom in and out to show them moving busily about the reef and then close-up so you can see their mouths, slower and more deliberate. The difference is the client fish wish to have their parasites removed, and these clients are parted with money, which I assume they want to keep although in the show they always make a big deal out of not counting dollars, while it seems here we are endlessly counting parasites.)

Everything Deeper, Darker

We return to the same places:
Palfrey, Mermaid, Vickis, Horseshoe,
spend an hour arguing over false entrances
on the way to the Bombie.

I am eclipsed by sameness,
or by the way nothing in the ocean
stays still but is always darting
to the periphery.

                    At Entrance,
my husband straps on his Shark Shield
which follows like the long barb
of the pink whiptail ray
we see later in the lagoon
down too deep for colours
and recognisable only by length.

Despite the shield we see one, two,
white tips beyond the shallow confines
of coral and sediment we keep to.

It is silent, but it is never silent,
the constant whistle of air across snorkel,
the slight choke of salt water down throat,
the cocoons of our bodies
expanding and cracking as we rise
from bottom to surface.

Yet we never hear or sense
the things around us, bar the parrot and puffer fish
knocking eagerly at the algae.

I wouldn't know what the threat was,
such bright colours on the eels
and undulating up and down the octopus,

while the shark wears the skin of the ocean
on a cloudy day, barely perceptible
but definitely there.

I am getting sick of the cleaner fish,
this island, the pain
in my shoulders, my ankle;
how every day brings a new injury
to my small patch of sand

                                    & this is the crux

here is no flag to be planted,
no species to be named,
nothing your scope can pinpoint
& you are men moving on fins
aimlessly in the water

                            I may be land

bound but I am steady & I call
it down for the nameless

                            I am ready

for the wind to pick up,
the boats to be loosed from their moorings,
for the new cyclone shelter to falter,

                            for you to be exposed

when every part of me is ripe
& ready for flight.

South Island

We go with our new housemates
to inspect the midden they've been digging
since July.
                        It's 1 m × 1 m at top
boarded by 4 rulers and pieces of strong wire.
It looks like a frame
for an absent picture
that might have hung
in a regional art gallery
since the '80s.

One of them squats in the hole
or bends at the waist and tries
to erase the sand binding the shells to time.
They get down 5 cm on a good day,
come back sunburned and dirty
even if that day they just sat – outside the pit
and mark with the plumbob and clipboard
where the shells had sunk.

The day before, on the verandah,
my husband and I read our books
and questioned what it means to dig.

I think it's like prayer;
the slow doing and undoing of a mandala,
while he thinks it's more propulsive –
the astronaut's curiosity to find out what's next.

The team leader takes us across
what he terms 'stable boulders'
to a headland high on the other beach side
where we face the outer reef.
Two dugongs and a shark swim past.

Here, he says, are stone arrangements
and there are cairns, stacks of rocks
which look not so much built as fashioned.
How deep the pit goes suggests
1000s more years of humans
than happenstance allows.

One pile of rocks he points to,
 saying, 'We think that's a turtle,'
and I wouldn't have known it
as anything but stones.
He indicates a head and then flippers,
as if he'd moved back from a large canvas
letting the whole come into view.

When we get back to the pit,
I ask the hunched shoulders
of the one digging, what it feels like to dig,
if it's faith or fear or some more human thing
and he says, 'Mate, it just feels
like sweat pouring off me'

and goes back to taking the sharpened chisel
to the calcified stone
beneath all our feet.

The Cleaner Fish Will Never Be Mythic

would die alongside Achilles but not be mourned
would watch Herakles from the distant shore and sigh
maybe one would be sacrificed to the Minotaur
on a neap tide but would not be written about

Jason would step over their bones at the bottom
of the labyrinth, claim the fleece and leave
they would gather at the back of feasts
in the temples, lay the pyres and wait
for their time to be called

                oh my
cleaners your name only sounds like a drum
when it is said rapidly in a Romance language
peixe limpadon   for a second you are not the crowd
but the word of the crowd, the chant
you are called and calling   you are loved
and ready to die

When the dolphins surface
right where I tell my husband
I see nothing,

the skipper turns to me and says,
'You should be able to get a poem
from that'

          In truth
I haven't thought
of writing today.

I lie listening to dead voices
ululate, the planes flying four times
overhead. Nothing lines up.

The book on my lap preaches
romance in long sentences
with adjectives two-by-two

in double barrelled shots. I don't
miss you but I miss thinking
I might. I always knew you

as one for whom words are easy
and what they promise, less. You are
on another island now. In the photo

you send, a bed big enough for three.
Yesterday I woke my husband at 7am
and asked him to be inside me, quickly.

Today I can't raise the strength to get
the 200m across sand to what passes
for civilisation. At least the weather

is consistent. The sun
burns and the wind comes up in afternoons
the way it should, even if

it doesn't die down at night
but keeps howling like something large
that never lands.

Tiago Sings Porto Songs

Sometimes a writer will use excessive repetition
to signal the intensification of some affect.
In her book *Mouthful of Green Plums*
Herta Muller depicts life under fascism using:
plums, a barber, strands of hair, a rabbit and a suitcase.

This is not how Tiago sings Porto songs.

Which he does, every day, for hours.
Even under water, Tiago sings Porto songs
and films himself fist pumping the fish,
taking out his regulator so we can see his mouth
'*Olé, Olé, Olé, Olé*' and 'Porto, Porto'.
There is nothing that expands or contracts
in these moments. He counts the fish
singing Porto, he does the dishes singing Porto
and he waits to call his kids with '*Olé, Olé, Olé, Olé.*'

Often, I've wondered what it takes
to be happy. When he is not singing Porto songs,
sometimes Tiago will ask Jose and I 'are you happy
with your lives' with that dropped final syllable
that says he is sure we are, like he is sure
Porto is the best football team, in the best country.
I'm not saying this to be sarcastic or gruesome

but this is a man I would skin and wear as a coat,
if it might ward away all that unshaped dark
with a chorus of Porto and a round of *Olé*.

Wrong Date

My new housemate is a surgeon
and is volunteering to pull weeds,
she shuffle-walks and doesn't bother me
when I sit still as a crumbling statue at my poems.
I ask her questions sometimes:
what happens to the nerve
when the tooth falls out, but
I get distracted by images darting
like damsels in staghorn, how
the nerve cannot flail like a worm
pushing up from a garden,
and it cannot know anything
including if it's alive.
We move between past and present
only through a connection to the future,
until that snaps and maybe
we just fade back
beyond the ovary
and even the nail-sized cell mass
to the thought in the brain,
which the surgeon tells me
still requires two things:
cells and electricity.

The New Girl Can't Kill the Fish

i.

She's come to know him, love him.
I've been waiting for this moment
after the routine beheadings and disembowlings,
waiting for someone to say 'stop'
'you can't' with all the theatre
of a soon-to-be-widow by the gallows,
although this is not that movie
and he still ends up dead.

After he is dead
she tends to him carefully,
still pressed up against
some greater emotion,
her back held straight by it,
her scalpel steady.

When the brain emerges
from the toothpick skull
like a squashed slug,
she allows herself to cry
and to begin to ferment something sour
which in time becomes resentment
for having been made to care at all.

ii.

In the end
she does not
kill the rest
but leaves them
with caretakers
so she can bring
an expert with her
in one month
someone for whom
extracting the pellet
of brain
is as easy as
clearing
a mousetrap
and who will teach her
how to separate
the smallest parts
like dissembling
a word
into unsayable
phonemes.

iii.

The surgeon tells me fish –
evolutionarily speaking – are now thought
to have been land creatures
that returned to the deep.

This does not make separating their parts easier
only more knowable,
like dissecting your own image
on the converse side
of a spoon.

iv.

When the surgeon loses patients
to less than ideal outcomes,
she makes sure to remember them
once-a-week riding her bike
up the hill on the outskirts
where she imagines the grass
bisected into a puzzle of graves. I ask,
if she ever gets stuck on
what to put on the tombstones,
she doesn't, just keeps riding,
but admits some haunt her more than others:
the 86 year old who, in prep,
said if there was a chance she could die
to leave the surgery unfinished
and then, in the heart of the op
her own stopped. Those,
she says, stick with you.

v.

I think the key with everything
is numbers. I write so many poems
but the bad ones fade –
at least from my memory –
and the act of writing has an ease
like reaching for a familiar light switch
upon returning home.
There is everything clinical
to the finished poem – like the body
sewn up or the fish pithed,
smothered or culled, the useful
parts retained and the rest frozen
in ziplock bags to be sent
back to Cairns on the next barge.

The Treatment Phase

is the midway between catch and results.
I think it is a part of the experiment
but apparently only the testing counts,
that – and what we do with it.
One of my subjects says
they don't want any more poems
written about them.
I'm not sure it is a result
or part of the conditioning.
I watch all the segments of the green-ant walk
along the green bench, the wind
raising the imported grasses
soaked in diesel into a higher fire
that just might catch the trees above.
The thing is, when they kill the fish,
there's no asking, although
sometimes there is a feeling
threatening to spread through the lab
which is not entirely unlike grief.

The three flippered turtle
     swims straight at your head
     attitude like *WHAT?*

Young even though its scars have calcified
     from when it swam the seas
with teenage insouciance

It just sits on the rock
     above the manta's cleaning station
with its hooked beak
and both its eyes
pointing this way

All the underwater creatures
     could not give a fuck

And we keep very carefully negotiating our tubes
and checking our gauges for the ability to float

In the light the tropical fish
     and nudebranchs
         are garish as Northbridge sex shops

The water XXX hot enough
     to mean just a shorty suit
         the currents fumbling at your joints
         like drunken fingers

Us staying low to avoid the drift
       that doesn't touch the turtle
and through which the smaller things slip easily

while we sink back-to-back
with the metal corpse
      we need to survive
amidst all that colour

I Make No Apologies

'I make no apologies for putting microorganisms on a pedestal above
all other living things. For if the last Blue Whale choked to death on
the last panda, it would be disastrous but not the end of the world'
Tom Curtis (July 2006) in *Nature Reviews Microbiology*.

The girl, 18, hops out the boat,
squeals to see a turtle.
There's nothing wrong with this of course,
nor that she likes turtles
because once on a Caribbean cruise
a man, 20, asked her to go on a turtle snorkel with him
and then to his room.

The slightest glimpse of a dugong
from atop the cliffs where it is
just cream in a coffee cloud
is more exciting than caffeine,
or the boy I thought I loved at 18,
glancing my hand against mine
as we dallied in the stockroom.

We all have things we love
because we are told to love them,
and things we love we shouldn't,
but what binds us are the things we should
love but don't because they are too small,
unsightly, unsighted, or when sighted

under a scope we only know enough to note
the shapes, like children learning their blocks.
Only them they love, place their sticky contours
from their hands to their mouths,
mostly wordless but coming to know
the feel of it, the taste.

But whether you can change a fish
is more uncertain, even if it
occupies only the final lines
of the discussion section
on how more species might be preserved
once the loss or expulsion
of the zooxanthellae leaves
only the skeleton of coral
to be covered by turf algae
before next year's cyclones
breaks it all down to browny-greenish rubble.
Intra- and inter- species relations
must be altered, communities formed
in denser bundles, predation
only for needs. Maybe the fish
can be taught independence,
to put some away for the next season
of warmer and warmer tides.
In experiments they paste
pictures of coral at different degrees
of degradation to the aquarium sides
like a house make-under show
or perhaps those people who learn
to live in one room or collect in one jar
their entire waste for a year.
I'm sorry for the tone of my voice.
Some things can not be changed.
As the paper is titled: *Aggressive*
females become aggressive males
in sex-changing reef fish. Like them
I must maintain my competitive advantage.

Closer

They changed the pH of the tanks,

the control's been running long enough
the experimental groups can start.

No great difference, a drop of .04.
And still I miss you.

Each day I tell my tongue: be light.
I've reduced things from my diet.

Red berries I read makes a woman sweeter.
After my iron infusion, I waited for the taste of blood

to come into my mouth with a wet redness,
and thought of the first Ripley book

where he quite patently loves Dickie
even as he paddles him off the boat.

Is this enough information to let you know
I still love you enough to bury you at sea?

But you haven't thought of me in months.
Brother, maybe the sea will be acid enough

that, after it takes the fish, it'll break us
and at least then I'll be sweeter

than what's left on the earth.

It's a Problem of Too Much Light

i. Overcast sunset

With the clouds overhead
the gradations of colour –
reef, sand and grass – stay
but take a softer turn.

What you have to watch for
is a colour that pierces.

When the coral bleaches
toothpaste-ad white,
the damselfish that stay
within 1m of their particular
garden of thorns for life
must choose to leave or die.

The nature of decay is patchy.
If, across the sand, living coral
is home to the same species
our fish can travel, if not
others will chase it back
onto the polished white teeth.

The softer colours of coral
and fish survive a little longer
from heat and from the bigger fish
which strike more against the yellow damsel
darting against the white coral
like a firefly among the dry drought wheat.

ii. Corals Do Not Need Reefs

The only thing coral needs
is herbivorous fish
to clean it of algae
and to whom it offers a home.
No one is sure whether the fish
need the coral more
than the coral needs them,
but it's clear
that there's nothing
which does not need,
and for whom there is something
which if taken away
leads to the slow decline
we all feel
when placed in a windowless room
with doors shut airtight
left only to breathe
what we ourselves
exhale.

iii. Coral Larvae are Fussy

and will not settle
on just any reef
particularly not those
substantially degraded
on which we find
high levels of bacterial slime.

South, my friend waits out her womb
hoping what she shoots
each day into her arm
will force a ripening
a settling.

But suppose it does
and is birthed into the world
in a pile of colour
like coral gametes seen from above,

will it know itself
having been grown
and tended for some more
temperate garden,

or will it be happy
to mistake the red algae
oil-slicked across the reef
for the LED-screen of colour

old photos prove the reef
can be.

iv. In the Turrell Exhibition at the NGA

you are led into a room
and saturated in a single colour.

At first, it's as though you descend
into an ink well, until
your optic centre resets

and everything becomes white.
The shadows of the others change
into high noon arcs you can't see

the origin of. It reminds you
of how on the reef
the zooxanthellae producing oxygen

at a rate beyond what the coral can consume,
glow brighter and brighter
until the oxygen

becomes poison instead of food.
Then, just when you think you've never seen
anything so beautiful,

so vibrant, the choking coral
will slough it all off like Joseph
giving up the technicolour dream coat

revealing all his blinding white flesh
to the sun.

v. What of the Soft Pink?

I notice the diver take one glove off,
stop to touch the fringes of the coral,

so I do the same: it is soft
like newly-laundered carpet

or how your voice was
in the one recording where we speak audibly.

I read your emails during quiet hours,
find in them pastel tones that don't translate

in the granite of my accent, the colour
of this ink. I guess I'd thought it

the most powerful and palatable
as what the squid and octopus eject

in a haze of fog that reveals you
as you are – solid – but how

much more forgiving the light colours are
how little they demand, how ready

they are to be touched.

vi. Let Me Sketch For You

a mountain, or rather
a granite outcrop with a small beach
to the northside. I am opposite it
on another island,
another sandy beach,
another day easy in the water.
The clouds today
are moving too fast
and the sun shines directly
on us all. Myself,
the bottom, the coral,
the fish emerging
from the rocks. One way
the bleaching occurs is this:
no cover, straight on,
too-warm currents
and a still day. Yet
if there is bliss
this is it, staring
away from the mainland
to where, out past the ribbon reef,
the shelf drops directly
into deep coral sea.

What's the Difference Between a Track and a Path

There are two ways
to travel the circumpolar current:
with the cold along the bottom
or up with the warmth,
eventually, though, to return
to your starting point
you must face the other water.

The current has only existed
since the Tethys sea died in the Late Miocene
and the Drake Passage opened,
which at 10 million years ago,
feels long enough to mean something,

exactly what we are still learning
along with what caused the Permian Extinction.
We're unlikely to learn it
before the water takes us back.

There Will Probably Still Be Music As We Go

a return to the lyre Hermes found

walking on a rotting mythic beach

and stubbing his toe against the remains

of a turtle, idly turning it

and proceeding to strum the exposed

taut muscle, the sound reverbing

against the hollow of the shell

For Once There is Not a Sunset of Some Beauty

Just me and two
beach thick-nees
walking and chirping
at the dark.

I say these are
my favourite birds
for the way they
continue ahead of you
skipping fast
rather than taking to flight.

They do not mind
the pedestrian.
At twilight
I find it almost possible
to see shapes on
the underside of
their seldom raised wings.

Some would call them pretty
as the dusk descends
but I say
what they are
is almost a
language of shadows

hidden
when the sun
insists on turning the sky
into a riot
of easy colour.

What else do you want to say
about this half-setting sun,
the seagull flown in from the boat?

Just like that it's over,
your hair is out
and it blows across your eyes
as you are writing this.

In the lab Jose and Tiago
triangulate an ectoparasite
under the lens
of an $80,000 microscope.

You like the ocean
for its lack of contours.
You are romantic like this.

The show you watch on your laptop
has one of those men
women are always falling for;
one with many locked boxes
and twisted circuitry.

You know there is a tone of voice
that will make him run right
but it's not among
the many voices you use
to smooth out the world.

Inside the lab, the bug is coming
slowly into focus. You cannot see it
but know it has six legs
and that there is a word for it
you are too mulish to learn.

Here again, there is a problem of voice.
Your hair is tangling
in the eastern trade winds

against the taffy-coloured
remnants of the day.

The fire is already laid
in the bbq pit
and if you wait

soon everyone will put down
their instruments for supper
and the silent sharing of flesh.

After He Edits My Poems, Jose Says My Voice Doesn't Sounds Like My Voice

i.

I sit on the deck and watch the island
be the island, the tree the tree,
the little red and green hummingbird
flit to the wire and away again.

I think about what it means
to be still. The aquifer
that supplies this salt place,
under the ground, dark and sweet,

only gains its warmth
when it travels up, is held
close to the light for a while.
Water feels nothing, parts easily,

allows what enters to move through.
But that is not the whole of it.
A dream I have often
is to dive down, lie on the bottom

where only a crescent of sun
reaches my face, even if
the force of all those small simple bonds
together, might suffocate.

ii.

Later I sit on the other couch
and focus on the silence
coming over like a cloud bank,
playing one of the old songs
that helps me make words
from feelings, as if I'm scoring the day:

the trip out to the mangroves
and then the hike to where
one coconut beach stretches straight
and inaccessible below us.

I keep still, catching the parts of me
that flutter, pinning them down.
There is no room among the brown limbs
and rapid syllables for anything
that might come unstuck, fly off the boat
or tangle in the motor.

                        For a while
I soften my edges, hold tight
to the rope and lean back
into the noise, the mess, the day.
Never forgetting how the ocean
is spread all round us
like the white space
on the page. And under it,
further and fathomed in sand,
what's fresh and dark
still waiting.

I know what I want

in watching the client fish
suspended, tail down to the coral
mouth open to the surface.

You never think of fish as stationary,
but here is one balancing in the water,
pectoral fins open to sky.

Maybe I've had it all wrong?
Thinking of the cleaner fish, myself,
and how we function in greed

or hunger, the bright flash
of their sides, like the back of a moth
convincing others they're larger

than they are. You can hear
the bigger fish when they eat,
but the cleaners are silent

at the flanks of their clients,
when they move gently at the gills
and lower their heads into the mouth.

Suspended, both fish
look like they are drinking
or something more than that.

The only two dark shapes
against the dense silence
of blue. Back at the lab

I write *eu sinto*
sua falta in blue
on the lab white board

and stay a little
in the empty space, focussing
on what my lips do

when I breathe

Notes

Three books were invaluable in the preparation of this manuscript:

Great Barrier Reef Marine Park Authority, *Interim Report: 2016 Coral Bleaching Event on the Great Barrier Reef.* Townsville: Great Barrier Reef Marine Park Authority, 2016.

Johnson J. E. and Marshall P. A. (editors), *Climate Change and the Great Barrier Reef.* Townsville: Great Barrier Reef Marine Park Authority and Australian Greenhouse Office, 2007.

Vernon, J. E. N, *A Reef in Time: The Great Barrier Reef from Beginning to End.* Cambridge, MA: Belknapp Press, 2008.

Individual poems reference and draw upon the following sources:

The section title 'What Makes a Cleaner a Cleaner?' is drawn from the title of S. Gingins' 2016 PhD Thesis submitted at the University of Neuchatel.

'Methods' –

> Grutter, A. S., 'Cleaner fish use tactile dancing behaviour as a preconflict management strategy', *Current Biology,* 14: 1080–1083, 2004.

'I Tell Tiago My Oldest Heartbreak Over Lunch' –

> Cote, I. M and K. L. Cheney, 'Choosing When to Be A Cleaner Fish Mimic', *Nature,* 433: 211, 2005.

'Female Cleaners are More Cooperative with Unfamiliar Males' – Bshary, R. and A. S. Grutter, 'Asymmetric Cheating Opportunities and Partner Control',*Animal Behaviour*, 63: 547–555, 2002.

'Asymmetric Partnership Arrangements' – Nichola J. Raihani, Ana I. Pinto, Alexandra S. Grutter, Sharon Wisner and Redouan Bshary, 'Male Cleaner Wrasses Adjust Punishment of Female Partners According to the stakes', *Proceedings of the Royal Society of Biology*, doi:10,1098/ rspb.2010.0690, pp. 1–6, 2011.

'You Can't Change a Man' – Sprenger, D., N. J. Dingemanse, N. A. Dochtermann, J. Theobald and S. P. W. Walker, 'Aggressive females become aggressive males in sex-changing reef fish', *Ecology Letters,* 15, pp. 986–992, 2012.

'Other Fish Aren't Capable of Feeding Against Their Preference' – Grutter, A. S. and R. Bshary, 'Cleaner Fish, Labroides Dimidiatus, Diet Preferences for different types of mucus and parasitic gnathiid isopods', *Animal Behaviour,* 68:583–588, 2004.

'The Cleaner Fish Will Never Be Mythic' – Pinto, A., J. Oates, A Grutter and R. Bshary, 'Cleaner Wrasses Labroides Dimidiatus Are More Cooperative in the Presence of An Audience', *Current Biology,* 21: 1140–1144, 2011.

'From What We Have Come to Sea' – 'section ix' data is sourced from page 40 of *A Reef in Time.* Anecdotal evidence from long-term residents and visitors at Lizard Island, however, suggests a slower growth rate for acropora.

'Recruitment' –

Bono, James. 'Science, Discourse, and Literature: The Role/Rule of Metaphor in Science', *Literature and Science* edited by Stuart Peterfreund. Boston: Northeastern University Press, pp. 59–89, 1990.

'It's a Problem of Too Much Light' –

Section 'i': Coker, Darren,. Pratchett, Morgan and Philip L. Munday, 'Coral Bleaching and Habitat Degradation Increases Susceptibility to Predation for Coral-Dwelling Fishes', *Behavioural Ecology*, vol. 20, issue 6, pp. 1204–1210, 2009.
Section 'ii': subtitle taken from page 39 of *A Reef in Time*.
Section 'iii': I encountered the suggestion of laying a floating shade-cloth on page 209 of *A Reef in Time*.
Section 'v': references the 2015 Turrell Retrospective held at the National Gallery of Australia

'Blue Carbon' –

Waycott, Michelle *et al.*, 'Vulnerability of seagrasses in the GBR to climate change' in Johnson J. E. and Marshall P. A. (editors) (2007*), Climate Change and the Great Barrier Reef.* Great Barrier Reef Marine Park Authority and Australian Greenhouse Office, pp. 193–235

Acknowledgements

First thanks to the team at Lizard Island Research Station: Anne, Lyle, Marianne and John; the work y'all do has nourished that patch of reef for decades. Particular love to Jose and Tiago for allowing a poet to tagalong on their fieldwork, and to the other researchers who allowed me into their worlds: I'm in awe of what you do. Charlie Maling and Colin Hill were great company and research assistants.

Thanks to Terri-ann White and the indefatigable team at UWAP, including the judges of the 2020 Dorothy Hewett Award for highly commending this manuscript and setting it on the path to publication. As always thanks to Judy Beveridge for her considered editorial voice. Omar Sakr was kind enough to read and comment on an early version of this manuscript. Georgia Richter and Catherine Noske provided valuable counsel.

Individual poems from this collection were first published in *Island*, *Australian Poetry Journal* and the Newcastle Poetry Prize 2019 anthology. This project was supported thanks to a grant from the Australia Council and the Marten Bequest in poetry.

As always I couldn't do the work I do without my family and friends.